I0005203

NAME: _____

PHONE: _____

MOBILE: _____

EMAIL: _____

ADDRESS: _____

A

SITE NAME:	URL:
USERNAME:	PASSWORD:
EMAIL ADDRESS:	
NOTES / SECURITY QUESTIONS:	

SITE NAME:	URL:
USERNAME:	PASSWORD:
EMAIL ADDRESS:	
NOTES / SECURITY QUESTIONS:	

SITE NAME:	URL:
USERNAME:	PASSWORD:
EMAIL ADDRESS:	
NOTES / SECURITY QUESTIONS:	

SITE NAME:	URL:
USERNAME:	PASSWORD:
EMAIL ADDRESS:	
NOTES / SECURITY QUESTIONS:	

A

SITE NAME:	URL:
USERNAME:	PASSWORD:
EMAIL ADDRESS:	
NOTES / SECURITY QUESTIONS:	

SITE NAME:	URL:
USERNAME:	PASSWORD:
EMAIL ADDRESS:	
NOTES / SECURITY QUESTIONS:	

SITE NAME:	URL:
USERNAME:	PASSWORD:
EMAIL ADDRESS:	
NOTES / SECURITY QUESTIONS:	

SITE NAME:	URL:
USERNAME:	PASSWORD:
EMAIL ADDRESS:	
NOTES / SECURITY QUESTIONS:	

A

SITE NAME:	URL:
USERNAME:	PASSWORD:
EMAIL ADDRESS:	
NOTES / SECURITY QUESTIONS:	

SITE NAME:	URL:
USERNAME:	PASSWORD:
EMAIL ADDRESS:	
NOTES / SECURITY QUESTIONS:	

SITE NAME:	URL:
USERNAME:	PASSWORD:
EMAIL ADDRESS:	
NOTES / SECURITY QUESTIONS:	

SITE NAME:	URL:
USERNAME:	PASSWORD:
EMAIL ADDRESS:	
NOTES / SECURITY QUESTIONS:	

A

SITE NAME:	URL:
USERNAME:	PASSWORD:
EMAIL ADDRESS:	
NOTES / SECURITY QUESTIONS:	

SITE NAME:	URL:
USERNAME:	PASSWORD:
EMAIL ADDRESS:	
NOTES / SECURITY QUESTIONS:	

SITE NAME:	URL:
USERNAME:	PASSWORD:
EMAIL ADDRESS:	
NOTES / SECURITY QUESTIONS:	

SITE NAME:	URL:
USERNAME:	PASSWORD:
EMAIL ADDRESS:	
NOTES / SECURITY QUESTIONS:	

B

SITE NAME:	URL:
USERNAME:	PASSWORD:
EMAIL ADDRESS:	
NOTES / SECURITY QUESTIONS:	

SITE NAME:	URL:
USERNAME:	PASSWORD:
EMAIL ADDRESS:	
NOTES / SECURITY QUESTIONS:	

SITE NAME:	URL:
USERNAME:	PASSWORD:
EMAIL ADDRESS:	
NOTES / SECURITY QUESTIONS:	

SITE NAME:	URL:
USERNAME:	PASSWORD:
EMAIL ADDRESS:	
NOTES / SECURITY QUESTIONS:	

B

SITE NAME:	URL:
USERNAME:	PASSWORD:
EMAIL ADDRESS:	
NOTES / SECURITY QUESTIONS:	

SITE NAME:	URL:
USERNAME:	PASSWORD:
EMAIL ADDRESS:	
NOTES / SECURITY QUESTIONS:	

SITE NAME:	URL:
USERNAME:	PASSWORD:
EMAIL ADDRESS:	
NOTES / SECURITY QUESTIONS:	

SITE NAME:	URL:
USERNAME:	PASSWORD:
EMAIL ADDRESS:	
NOTES / SECURITY QUESTIONS:	

B

SITE NAME:	URL:
USERNAME:	PASSWORD:
EMAIL ADDRESS:	
NOTES / SECURITY QUESTIONS:	

SITE NAME:	URL:
USERNAME:	PASSWORD:
EMAIL ADDRESS:	
NOTES / SECURITY QUESTIONS:	

SITE NAME:	URL:
USERNAME:	PASSWORD:
EMAIL ADDRESS:	
NOTES / SECURITY QUESTIONS:	

SITE NAME:	URL:
USERNAME:	PASSWORD:
EMAIL ADDRESS:	
NOTES / SECURITY QUESTIONS:	

B

SITE NAME:	URL:
USERNAME:	PASSWORD:
EMAIL ADDRESS:	
NOTES / SECURITY QUESTIONS:	

SITE NAME:	URL:
USERNAME:	PASSWORD:
EMAIL ADDRESS:	
NOTES / SECURITY QUESTIONS:	

SITE NAME:	URL:
USERNAME:	PASSWORD:
EMAIL ADDRESS:	
NOTES / SECURITY QUESTIONS:	

SITE NAME:	URL:
USERNAME:	PASSWORD:
EMAIL ADDRESS:	
NOTES / SECURITY QUESTIONS:	

C

SITE NAME:	URL:
USERNAME:	PASSWORD:
EMAIL ADDRESS:	
NOTES / SECURITY QUESTIONS:	

SITE NAME:	URL:
USERNAME:	PASSWORD:
EMAIL ADDRESS:	
NOTES / SECURITY QUESTIONS:	

SITE NAME:	URL:
USERNAME:	PASSWORD:
EMAIL ADDRESS:	
NOTES / SECURITY QUESTIONS:	

SITE NAME:	URL:
USERNAME:	PASSWORD:
EMAIL ADDRESS:	
NOTES / SECURITY QUESTIONS:	

C

SITE NAME:	URL:
USERNAME:	PASSWORD:
EMAIL ADDRESS:	
NOTES / SECURITY QUESTIONS:	

SITE NAME:	URL:
USERNAME:	PASSWORD:
EMAIL ADDRESS:	
NOTES / SECURITY QUESTIONS:	

SITE NAME:	URL:
USERNAME:	PASSWORD:
EMAIL ADDRESS:	
NOTES / SECURITY QUESTIONS:	

SITE NAME:	URL:
USERNAME:	PASSWORD:
EMAIL ADDRESS:	
NOTES / SECURITY QUESTIONS:	

C

SITE NAME:	URL:
USERNAME:	PASSWORD:
EMAIL ADDRESS:	
NOTES / SECURITY QUESTIONS:	

SITE NAME:	URL:
USERNAME:	PASSWORD:
EMAIL ADDRESS:	
NOTES / SECURITY QUESTIONS:	

SITE NAME:	URL:
USERNAME:	PASSWORD:
EMAIL ADDRESS:	
NOTES / SECURITY QUESTIONS:	

SITE NAME:	URL:
USERNAME:	PASSWORD:
EMAIL ADDRESS:	
NOTES / SECURITY QUESTIONS:	

C

SITE NAME:	URL:
USERNAME:	PASSWORD:
EMAIL ADDRESS:	
NOTES / SECURITY QUESTIONS:	

SITE NAME:	URL:
USERNAME:	PASSWORD:
EMAIL ADDRESS:	
NOTES / SECURITY QUESTIONS:	

SITE NAME:	URL:
USERNAME:	PASSWORD:
EMAIL ADDRESS:	
NOTES / SECURITY QUESTIONS:	

SITE NAME:	URL:
USERNAME:	PASSWORD:
EMAIL ADDRESS:	
NOTES / SECURITY QUESTIONS:	

D

SITE NAME:	URL:
USERNAME:	PASSWORD:
EMAIL ADDRESS:	
NOTES / SECURITY QUESTIONS:	

SITE NAME:	URL:
USERNAME:	PASSWORD:
EMAIL ADDRESS:	
NOTES / SECURITY QUESTIONS:	

SITE NAME:	URL:
USERNAME:	PASSWORD:
EMAIL ADDRESS:	
NOTES / SECURITY QUESTIONS:	

SITE NAME:	URL:
USERNAME:	PASSWORD:
EMAIL ADDRESS:	
NOTES / SECURITY QUESTIONS:	

D

SITE NAME:	URL:
USERNAME:	PASSWORD:
EMAIL ADDRESS:	
NOTES / SECURITY QUESTIONS:	

SITE NAME:	URL:
USERNAME:	PASSWORD:
EMAIL ADDRESS:	
NOTES / SECURITY QUESTIONS:	

SITE NAME:	URL:
USERNAME:	PASSWORD:
EMAIL ADDRESS:	
NOTES / SECURITY QUESTIONS:	

SITE NAME:	URL:
USERNAME:	PASSWORD:
EMAIL ADDRESS:	
NOTES / SECURITY QUESTIONS:	

D

SITE NAME:	URL:
USERNAME:	PASSWORD:
EMAIL ADDRESS:	
NOTES / SECURITY QUESTIONS:	

SITE NAME:	URL:
USERNAME:	PASSWORD:
EMAIL ADDRESS:	
NOTES / SECURITY QUESTIONS:	

SITE NAME:	URL:
USERNAME:	PASSWORD:
EMAIL ADDRESS:	
NOTES / SECURITY QUESTIONS:	

SITE NAME:	URL:
USERNAME:	PASSWORD:
EMAIL ADDRESS:	
NOTES / SECURITY QUESTIONS:	

D

SITE NAME:	URL:
USERNAME:	PASSWORD:
EMAIL ADDRESS:	
NOTES / SECURITY QUESTIONS:	

SITE NAME:	URL:
USERNAME:	PASSWORD:
EMAIL ADDRESS:	
NOTES / SECURITY QUESTIONS:	

SITE NAME:	URL:
USERNAME:	PASSWORD:
EMAIL ADDRESS:	
NOTES / SECURITY QUESTIONS:	

SITE NAME:	URL:
USERNAME:	PASSWORD:
EMAIL ADDRESS:	
NOTES / SECURITY QUESTIONS:	

E

SITE NAME:	URL:
USERNAME:	PASSWORD:
EMAIL ADDRESS:	
NOTES / SECURITY QUESTIONS:	

SITE NAME:	URL:
USERNAME:	PASSWORD:
EMAIL ADDRESS:	
NOTES / SECURITY QUESTIONS:	

SITE NAME:	URL:
USERNAME:	PASSWORD:
EMAIL ADDRESS:	
NOTES / SECURITY QUESTIONS:	

SITE NAME:	URL:
USERNAME:	PASSWORD:
EMAIL ADDRESS:	
NOTES / SECURITY QUESTIONS:	

E

SITE NAME:	URL:
USERNAME:	PASSWORD:
EMAIL ADDRESS:	
NOTES / SECURITY QUESTIONS:	

SITE NAME:	URL:
USERNAME:	PASSWORD:
EMAIL ADDRESS:	
NOTES / SECURITY QUESTIONS:	

SITE NAME:	URL:
USERNAME:	PASSWORD:
EMAIL ADDRESS:	
NOTES / SECURITY QUESTIONS:	

SITE NAME:	URL:
USERNAME:	PASSWORD:
EMAIL ADDRESS:	
NOTES / SECURITY QUESTIONS:	

E

SITE NAME:	URL:
USERNAME:	PASSWORD:
EMAIL ADDRESS:	
NOTES / SECURITY QUESTIONS:	

SITE NAME:	URL:
USERNAME:	PASSWORD:
EMAIL ADDRESS:	
NOTES / SECURITY QUESTIONS:	

SITE NAME:	URL:
USERNAME:	PASSWORD:
EMAIL ADDRESS:	
NOTES / SECURITY QUESTIONS:	

SITE NAME:	URL:
USERNAME:	PASSWORD:
EMAIL ADDRESS:	
NOTES / SECURITY QUESTIONS:	

E

SITE NAME:	URL:
USERNAME:	PASSWORD:
EMAIL ADDRESS:	
NOTES / SECURITY QUESTIONS:	

SITE NAME:	URL:
USERNAME:	PASSWORD:
EMAIL ADDRESS:	
NOTES / SECURITY QUESTIONS:	

SITE NAME:	URL:
USERNAME:	PASSWORD:
EMAIL ADDRESS:	
NOTES / SECURITY QUESTIONS:	

SITE NAME:	URL:
USERNAME:	PASSWORD:
EMAIL ADDRESS:	
NOTES / SECURITY QUESTIONS:	

F

SITE NAME:	URL:
USERNAME:	PASSWORD:
EMAIL ADDRESS:	
NOTES / SECURITY QUESTIONS:	

SITE NAME:	URL:
USERNAME:	PASSWORD:
EMAIL ADDRESS:	
NOTES / SECURITY QUESTIONS:	

SITE NAME:	URL:
USERNAME:	PASSWORD:
EMAIL ADDRESS:	
NOTES / SECURITY QUESTIONS:	

SITE NAME:	URL:
USERNAME:	PASSWORD:
EMAIL ADDRESS:	
NOTES / SECURITY QUESTIONS:	

F

SITE NAME:	URL:
USERNAME:	PASSWORD:
EMAIL ADDRESS:	
NOTES / SECURITY QUESTIONS:	

SITE NAME:	URL:
USERNAME:	PASSWORD:
EMAIL ADDRESS:	
NOTES / SECURITY QUESTIONS:	

SITE NAME:	URL:
USERNAME:	PASSWORD:
EMAIL ADDRESS:	
NOTES / SECURITY QUESTIONS:	

SITE NAME:	URL:
USERNAME:	PASSWORD:
EMAIL ADDRESS:	
NOTES / SECURITY QUESTIONS:	

F

SITE NAME:	URL:
USERNAME:	PASSWORD:
EMAIL ADDRESS:	
NOTES / SECURITY QUESTIONS:	

SITE NAME:	URL:
USERNAME:	PASSWORD:
EMAIL ADDRESS:	
NOTES / SECURITY QUESTIONS:	

SITE NAME:	URL:
USERNAME:	PASSWORD:
EMAIL ADDRESS:	
NOTES / SECURITY QUESTIONS:	

SITE NAME:	URL:
USERNAME:	PASSWORD:
EMAIL ADDRESS:	
NOTES / SECURITY QUESTIONS:	

F

SITE NAME:	URL:
USERNAME:	PASSWORD:
EMAIL ADDRESS:	
NOTES / SECURITY QUESTIONS:	

SITE NAME:	URL:
USERNAME:	PASSWORD:
EMAIL ADDRESS:	
NOTES / SECURITY QUESTIONS:	

SITE NAME:	URL:
USERNAME:	PASSWORD:
EMAIL ADDRESS:	
NOTES / SECURITY QUESTIONS:	

SITE NAME:	URL:
USERNAME:	PASSWORD:
EMAIL ADDRESS:	
NOTES / SECURITY QUESTIONS:	

G

SITE NAME:	URL:
USERNAME:	PASSWORD:
EMAIL ADDRESS:	
NOTES / SECURITY QUESTIONS:	

SITE NAME:	URL:
USERNAME:	PASSWORD:
EMAIL ADDRESS:	
NOTES / SECURITY QUESTIONS:	

SITE NAME:	URL:
USERNAME:	PASSWORD:
EMAIL ADDRESS:	
NOTES / SECURITY QUESTIONS:	

SITE NAME:	URL:
USERNAME:	PASSWORD:
EMAIL ADDRESS:	
NOTES / SECURITY QUESTIONS:	

G

SITE NAME:	URL:
USERNAME:	PASSWORD:
EMAIL ADDRESS:	
NOTES / SECURITY QUESTIONS:	

SITE NAME:	URL:
USERNAME:	PASSWORD:
EMAIL ADDRESS:	
NOTES / SECURITY QUESTIONS:	

SITE NAME:	URL:
USERNAME:	PASSWORD:
EMAIL ADDRESS:	
NOTES / SECURITY QUESTIONS:	

SITE NAME:	URL:
USERNAME:	PASSWORD:
EMAIL ADDRESS:	
NOTES / SECURITY QUESTIONS:	

G

SITE NAME:	URL:
USERNAME:	PASSWORD:
EMAIL ADDRESS:	
NOTES / SECURITY QUESTIONS:	

SITE NAME:	URL:
USERNAME:	PASSWORD:
EMAIL ADDRESS:	
NOTES / SECURITY QUESTIONS:	

SITE NAME:	URL:
USERNAME:	PASSWORD:
EMAIL ADDRESS:	
NOTES / SECURITY QUESTIONS:	

SITE NAME:	URL:
USERNAME:	PASSWORD:
EMAIL ADDRESS:	
NOTES / SECURITY QUESTIONS:	

G

SITE NAME:	URL:
USERNAME:	PASSWORD:
EMAIL ADDRESS:	
NOTES / SECURITY QUESTIONS:	

SITE NAME:	URL:
USERNAME:	PASSWORD:
EMAIL ADDRESS:	
NOTES / SECURITY QUESTIONS:	

SITE NAME:	URL:
USERNAME:	PASSWORD:
EMAIL ADDRESS:	
NOTES / SECURITY QUESTIONS:	

SITE NAME:	URL:
USERNAME:	PASSWORD:
EMAIL ADDRESS:	
NOTES / SECURITY QUESTIONS:	

H

SITE NAME:	URL:
USERNAME:	PASSWORD:
EMAIL ADDRESS:	
NOTES / SECURITY QUESTIONS:	

SITE NAME:	URL:
USERNAME:	PASSWORD:
EMAIL ADDRESS:	
NOTES / SECURITY QUESTIONS:	

SITE NAME:	URL:
USERNAME:	PASSWORD:
EMAIL ADDRESS:	
NOTES / SECURITY QUESTIONS:	

SITE NAME:	URL:
USERNAME:	PASSWORD:
EMAIL ADDRESS:	
NOTES / SECURITY QUESTIONS:	

H

SITE NAME:	URL:
USERNAME:	PASSWORD:
EMAIL ADDRESS:	
NOTES / SECURITY QUESTIONS:	

SITE NAME:	URL:
USERNAME:	PASSWORD:
EMAIL ADDRESS:	
NOTES / SECURITY QUESTIONS:	

SITE NAME:	URL:
USERNAME:	PASSWORD:
EMAIL ADDRESS:	
NOTES / SECURITY QUESTIONS:	

SITE NAME:	URL:
USERNAME:	PASSWORD:
EMAIL ADDRESS:	
NOTES / SECURITY QUESTIONS:	

H

SITE NAME:	URL:
USERNAME:	PASSWORD:
EMAIL ADDRESS:	
NOTES / SECURITY QUESTIONS:	

SITE NAME:	URL:
USERNAME:	PASSWORD:
EMAIL ADDRESS:	
NOTES / SECURITY QUESTIONS:	

SITE NAME:	URL:
USERNAME:	PASSWORD:
EMAIL ADDRESS:	
NOTES / SECURITY QUESTIONS:	

SITE NAME:	URL:
USERNAME:	PASSWORD:
EMAIL ADDRESS:	
NOTES / SECURITY QUESTIONS:	

H

SITE NAME:	URL:
USERNAME:	PASSWORD:
EMAIL ADDRESS:	
NOTES / SECURITY QUESTIONS:	

SITE NAME:	URL:
USERNAME:	PASSWORD:
EMAIL ADDRESS:	
NOTES / SECURITY QUESTIONS:	

SITE NAME:	URL:
USERNAME:	PASSWORD:
EMAIL ADDRESS:	
NOTES / SECURITY QUESTIONS:	

SITE NAME:	URL:
USERNAME:	PASSWORD:
EMAIL ADDRESS:	
NOTES / SECURITY QUESTIONS:	

SITE NAME:	URL:
USERNAME:	PASSWORD:
EMAIL ADDRESS:	
NOTES / SECURITY QUESTIONS:	

SITE NAME:	URL:
USERNAME:	PASSWORD:
EMAIL ADDRESS:	
NOTES / SECURITY QUESTIONS:	

SITE NAME:	URL:
USERNAME:	PASSWORD:
EMAIL ADDRESS:	
NOTES / SECURITY QUESTIONS:	

SITE NAME:	URL:
USERNAME:	PASSWORD:
EMAIL ADDRESS:	
NOTES / SECURITY QUESTIONS:	

SITE NAME:	URL:
USERNAME:	PASSWORD:
EMAIL ADDRESS:	
NOTES / SECURITY QUESTIONS:	

SITE NAME:	URL:
USERNAME:	PASSWORD:
EMAIL ADDRESS:	
NOTES / SECURITY QUESTIONS:	

SITE NAME:	URL:
USERNAME:	PASSWORD:
EMAIL ADDRESS:	
NOTES / SECURITY QUESTIONS:	

SITE NAME:	URL:
USERNAME:	PASSWORD:
EMAIL ADDRESS:	
NOTES / SECURITY QUESTIONS:	

SITE NAME:	URL:
USERNAME:	PASSWORD:
EMAIL ADDRESS:	
NOTES / SECURITY QUESTIONS:	

SITE NAME:	URL:
USERNAME:	PASSWORD:
EMAIL ADDRESS:	
NOTES / SECURITY QUESTIONS:	

SITE NAME:	URL:
USERNAME:	PASSWORD:
EMAIL ADDRESS:	
NOTES / SECURITY QUESTIONS:	

SITE NAME:	URL:
USERNAME:	PASSWORD:
EMAIL ADDRESS:	
NOTES / SECURITY QUESTIONS:	

SITE NAME:	URL:
USERNAME:	PASSWORD:
EMAIL ADDRESS:	
NOTES / SECURITY QUESTIONS:	

SITE NAME:	URL:
USERNAME:	PASSWORD:
EMAIL ADDRESS:	
NOTES / SECURITY QUESTIONS:	

SITE NAME:	URL:
USERNAME:	PASSWORD:
EMAIL ADDRESS:	
NOTES / SECURITY QUESTIONS:	

SITE NAME:	URL:
USERNAME:	PASSWORD:
EMAIL ADDRESS:	
NOTES / SECURITY QUESTIONS:	

J

SITE NAME:	URL:
USERNAME:	PASSWORD:
EMAIL ADDRESS:	
NOTES / SECURITY QUESTIONS:	

SITE NAME:	URL:
USERNAME:	PASSWORD:
EMAIL ADDRESS:	
NOTES / SECURITY QUESTIONS:	

SITE NAME:	URL:
USERNAME:	PASSWORD:
EMAIL ADDRESS:	
NOTES / SECURITY QUESTIONS:	

SITE NAME:	URL:
USERNAME:	PASSWORD:
EMAIL ADDRESS:	
NOTES / SECURITY QUESTIONS:	

J

SITE NAME:	URL:
USERNAME:	PASSWORD:
EMAIL ADDRESS:	
NOTES / SECURITY QUESTIONS:	

SITE NAME:	URL:
USERNAME:	PASSWORD:
EMAIL ADDRESS:	
NOTES / SECURITY QUESTIONS:	

SITE NAME:	URL:
USERNAME:	PASSWORD:
EMAIL ADDRESS:	
NOTES / SECURITY QUESTIONS:	

SITE NAME:	URL:
USERNAME:	PASSWORD:
EMAIL ADDRESS:	
NOTES / SECURITY QUESTIONS:	

J

SITE NAME:	URL:
USERNAME:	PASSWORD:
EMAIL ADDRESS:	
NOTES / SECURITY QUESTIONS:	

SITE NAME:	URL:
USERNAME:	PASSWORD:
EMAIL ADDRESS:	
NOTES / SECURITY QUESTIONS:	

SITE NAME:	URL:
USERNAME:	PASSWORD:
EMAIL ADDRESS:	
NOTES / SECURITY QUESTIONS:	

SITE NAME:	URL:
USERNAME:	PASSWORD:
EMAIL ADDRESS:	
NOTES / SECURITY QUESTIONS:	

J

SITE NAME:	URL:
USERNAME:	PASSWORD:
EMAIL ADDRESS:	
NOTES / SECURITY QUESTIONS:	

SITE NAME:	URL:
USERNAME:	PASSWORD:
EMAIL ADDRESS:	
NOTES / SECURITY QUESTIONS:	

SITE NAME:	URL:
USERNAME:	PASSWORD:
EMAIL ADDRESS:	
NOTES / SECURITY QUESTIONS:	

SITE NAME:	URL:
USERNAME:	PASSWORD:
EMAIL ADDRESS:	
NOTES / SECURITY QUESTIONS:	

K

SITE NAME:	URL:
USERNAME:	PASSWORD:
EMAIL ADDRESS:	
NOTES / SECURITY QUESTIONS:	

SITE NAME:	URL:
USERNAME:	PASSWORD:
EMAIL ADDRESS:	
NOTES / SECURITY QUESTIONS:	

SITE NAME:	URL:
USERNAME:	PASSWORD:
EMAIL ADDRESS:	
NOTES / SECURITY QUESTIONS:	

SITE NAME:	URL:
USERNAME:	PASSWORD:
EMAIL ADDRESS:	
NOTES / SECURITY QUESTIONS:	

K

SITE NAME:	URL:
USERNAME:	PASSWORD:
EMAIL ADDRESS:	
NOTES / SECURITY QUESTIONS:	

SITE NAME:	URL:
USERNAME:	PASSWORD:
EMAIL ADDRESS:	
NOTES / SECURITY QUESTIONS:	

SITE NAME:	URL:
USERNAME:	PASSWORD:
EMAIL ADDRESS:	
NOTES / SECURITY QUESTIONS:	

SITE NAME:	URL:
USERNAME:	PASSWORD:
EMAIL ADDRESS:	
NOTES / SECURITY QUESTIONS:	

K

SITE NAME:	URL:
USERNAME:	PASSWORD:
EMAIL ADDRESS:	
NOTES / SECURITY QUESTIONS:	

SITE NAME:	URL:
USERNAME:	PASSWORD:
EMAIL ADDRESS:	
NOTES / SECURITY QUESTIONS:	

SITE NAME:	URL:
USERNAME:	PASSWORD:
EMAIL ADDRESS:	
NOTES / SECURITY QUESTIONS:	

SITE NAME:	URL:
USERNAME:	PASSWORD:
EMAIL ADDRESS:	
NOTES / SECURITY QUESTIONS:	

K

SITE NAME:	URL:
USERNAME:	PASSWORD:
EMAIL ADDRESS:	
NOTES / SECURITY QUESTIONS:	

SITE NAME:	URL:
USERNAME:	PASSWORD:
EMAIL ADDRESS:	
NOTES / SECURITY QUESTIONS:	

SITE NAME:	URL:
USERNAME:	PASSWORD:
EMAIL ADDRESS:	
NOTES / SECURITY QUESTIONS:	

SITE NAME:	URL:
USERNAME:	PASSWORD:
EMAIL ADDRESS:	
NOTES / SECURITY QUESTIONS:	

L

SITE NAME:	URL:
USERNAME:	PASSWORD:
EMAIL ADDRESS:	
NOTES / SECURITY QUESTIONS:	

SITE NAME:	URL:
USERNAME:	PASSWORD:
EMAIL ADDRESS:	
NOTES / SECURITY QUESTIONS:	

SITE NAME:	URL:
USERNAME:	PASSWORD:
EMAIL ADDRESS:	
NOTES / SECURITY QUESTIONS:	

SITE NAME:	URL:
USERNAME:	PASSWORD:
EMAIL ADDRESS:	
NOTES / SECURITY QUESTIONS:	

L

SITE NAME:	URL:
USERNAME:	PASSWORD:
EMAIL ADDRESS:	
NOTES / SECURITY QUESTIONS:	

SITE NAME:	URL:
USERNAME:	PASSWORD:
EMAIL ADDRESS:	
NOTES / SECURITY QUESTIONS:	

SITE NAME:	URL:
USERNAME:	PASSWORD:
EMAIL ADDRESS:	
NOTES / SECURITY QUESTIONS:	

SITE NAME:	URL:
USERNAME:	PASSWORD:
EMAIL ADDRESS:	
NOTES / SECURITY QUESTIONS:	

L

SITE NAME:	URL:
USERNAME:	PASSWORD:
EMAIL ADDRESS:	
NOTES / SECURITY QUESTIONS:	

SITE NAME:	URL:
USERNAME:	PASSWORD:
EMAIL ADDRESS:	
NOTES / SECURITY QUESTIONS:	

SITE NAME:	URL:
USERNAME:	PASSWORD:
EMAIL ADDRESS:	
NOTES / SECURITY QUESTIONS:	

SITE NAME:	URL:
USERNAME:	PASSWORD:
EMAIL ADDRESS:	
NOTES / SECURITY QUESTIONS:	

L

SITE NAME:	URL:
USERNAME:	PASSWORD:
EMAIL ADDRESS:	
NOTES / SECURITY QUESTIONS:	

SITE NAME:	URL:
USERNAME:	PASSWORD:
EMAIL ADDRESS:	
NOTES / SECURITY QUESTIONS:	

SITE NAME:	URL:
USERNAME:	PASSWORD:
EMAIL ADDRESS:	
NOTES / SECURITY QUESTIONS:	

SITE NAME:	URL:
USERNAME:	PASSWORD:
EMAIL ADDRESS:	
NOTES / SECURITY QUESTIONS:	

M

SITE NAME:	URL:
USERNAME:	PASSWORD:
EMAIL ADDRESS:	
NOTES / SECURITY QUESTIONS:	

SITE NAME:	URL:
USERNAME:	PASSWORD:
EMAIL ADDRESS:	
NOTES / SECURITY QUESTIONS:	

SITE NAME:	URL:
USERNAME:	PASSWORD:
EMAIL ADDRESS:	
NOTES / SECURITY QUESTIONS:	

SITE NAME:	URL:
USERNAME:	PASSWORD:
EMAIL ADDRESS:	
NOTES / SECURITY QUESTIONS:	

M

SITE NAME:	URL:
USERNAME:	PASSWORD:
EMAIL ADDRESS:	
NOTES / SECURITY QUESTIONS:	

SITE NAME:	URL:
USERNAME:	PASSWORD:
EMAIL ADDRESS:	
NOTES / SECURITY QUESTIONS:	

SITE NAME:	URL:
USERNAME:	PASSWORD:
EMAIL ADDRESS:	
NOTES / SECURITY QUESTIONS:	

SITE NAME:	URL:
USERNAME:	PASSWORD:
EMAIL ADDRESS:	
NOTES / SECURITY QUESTIONS:	

M

SITE NAME:	URL:
USERNAME:	PASSWORD:
EMAIL ADDRESS:	
NOTES / SECURITY QUESTIONS:	

SITE NAME:	URL:
USERNAME:	PASSWORD:
EMAIL ADDRESS:	
NOTES / SECURITY QUESTIONS:	

SITE NAME:	URL:
USERNAME:	PASSWORD:
EMAIL ADDRESS:	
NOTES / SECURITY QUESTIONS:	

SITE NAME:	URL:
USERNAME:	PASSWORD:
EMAIL ADDRESS:	
NOTES / SECURITY QUESTIONS:	

M

SITE NAME:	URL:
USERNAME:	PASSWORD:
EMAIL ADDRESS:	
NOTES / SECURITY QUESTIONS:	

SITE NAME:	URL:
USERNAME:	PASSWORD:
EMAIL ADDRESS:	
NOTES / SECURITY QUESTIONS:	

SITE NAME:	URL:
USERNAME:	PASSWORD:
EMAIL ADDRESS:	
NOTES / SECURITY QUESTIONS:	

SITE NAME:	URL:
USERNAME:	PASSWORD:
EMAIL ADDRESS:	
NOTES / SECURITY QUESTIONS:	

N

SITE NAME:	URL:
USERNAME:	PASSWORD:
EMAIL ADDRESS:	
NOTES / SECURITY QUESTIONS:	

SITE NAME:	URL:
USERNAME:	PASSWORD:
EMAIL ADDRESS:	
NOTES / SECURITY QUESTIONS:	

SITE NAME:	URL:
USERNAME:	PASSWORD:
EMAIL ADDRESS:	
NOTES / SECURITY QUESTIONS:	

SITE NAME:	URL:
USERNAME:	PASSWORD:
EMAIL ADDRESS:	
NOTES / SECURITY QUESTIONS:	

N

SITE NAME: | **URL:**

USERNAME: | **PASSWORD:**

EMAIL ADDRESS:

NOTES / SECURITY QUESTIONS:

SITE NAME: | **URL:**

USERNAME: | **PASSWORD:**

EMAIL ADDRESS:

NOTES / SECURITY QUESTIONS:

SITE NAME: | **URL:**

USERNAME: | **PASSWORD:**

EMAIL ADDRESS:

NOTES / SECURITY QUESTIONS:

SITE NAME: | **URL:**

USERNAME: | **PASSWORD:**

EMAIL ADDRESS:

NOTES / SECURITY QUESTIONS:

N

SITE NAME:	URL:
USERNAME:	PASSWORD:
EMAIL ADDRESS:	
NOTES / SECURITY QUESTIONS:	

SITE NAME:	URL:
USERNAME:	PASSWORD:
EMAIL ADDRESS:	
NOTES / SECURITY QUESTIONS:	

SITE NAME:	URL:
USERNAME:	PASSWORD:
EMAIL ADDRESS:	
NOTES / SECURITY QUESTIONS:	

SITE NAME:	URL:
USERNAME:	PASSWORD:
EMAIL ADDRESS:	
NOTES / SECURITY QUESTIONS:	

N

SITE NAME:	URL:
USERNAME:	PASSWORD:
EMAIL ADDRESS:	
NOTES / SECURITY QUESTIONS:	

SITE NAME:	URL:
USERNAME:	PASSWORD:
EMAIL ADDRESS:	
NOTES / SECURITY QUESTIONS:	

SITE NAME:	URL:
USERNAME:	PASSWORD:
EMAIL ADDRESS:	
NOTES / SECURITY QUESTIONS:	

SITE NAME:	URL:
USERNAME:	PASSWORD:
EMAIL ADDRESS:	
NOTES / SECURITY QUESTIONS:	

(O)

SITE NAME: | **URL:**

USERNAME: | **PASSWORD:**

EMAIL ADDRESS:

NOTES / SECURITY QUESTIONS:

SITE NAME: | **URL:**

USERNAME: | **PASSWORD:**

EMAIL ADDRESS:

NOTES / SECURITY QUESTIONS:

SITE NAME: | **URL:**

USERNAME: | **PASSWORD:**

EMAIL ADDRESS:

NOTES / SECURITY QUESTIONS:

SITE NAME: | **URL:**

USERNAME: | **PASSWORD:**

EMAIL ADDRESS:

NOTES / SECURITY QUESTIONS:

O

SITE NAME:	URL:
USERNAME:	PASSWORD:
EMAIL ADDRESS:	
NOTES / SECURITY QUESTIONS:	

SITE NAME:	URL:
USERNAME:	PASSWORD:
EMAIL ADDRESS:	
NOTES / SECURITY QUESTIONS:	

SITE NAME:	URL:
USERNAME:	PASSWORD:
EMAIL ADDRESS:	
NOTES / SECURITY QUESTIONS:	

SITE NAME:	URL:
USERNAME:	PASSWORD:
EMAIL ADDRESS:	
NOTES / SECURITY QUESTIONS:	

(0)

SITE NAME:	URL:
USERNAME:	PASSWORD:
EMAIL ADDRESS:	
NOTES / SECURITY QUESTIONS:	

SITE NAME:	URL:
USERNAME:	PASSWORD:
EMAIL ADDRESS:	
NOTES / SECURITY QUESTIONS:	

SITE NAME:	URL:
USERNAME:	PASSWORD:
EMAIL ADDRESS:	
NOTES / SECURITY QUESTIONS:	

SITE NAME:	URL:
USERNAME:	PASSWORD:
EMAIL ADDRESS:	
NOTES / SECURITY QUESTIONS:	

SITE NAME:	URL:
USERNAME:	PASSWORD:
EMAIL ADDRESS:	
NOTES / SECURITY QUESTIONS:	

SITE NAME:	URL:
USERNAME:	PASSWORD:
EMAIL ADDRESS:	
NOTES / SECURITY QUESTIONS:	

SITE NAME:	URL:
USERNAME:	PASSWORD:
EMAIL ADDRESS:	
NOTES / SECURITY QUESTIONS:	

SITE NAME:	URL:
USERNAME:	PASSWORD:
EMAIL ADDRESS:	
NOTES / SECURITY QUESTIONS:	

P

SITE NAME:	URL:
USERNAME:	PASSWORD:
EMAIL ADDRESS:	
NOTES / SECURITY QUESTIONS:	

SITE NAME:	URL:
USERNAME:	PASSWORD:
EMAIL ADDRESS:	
NOTES / SECURITY QUESTIONS:	

SITE NAME:	URL:
USERNAME:	PASSWORD:
EMAIL ADDRESS:	
NOTES / SECURITY QUESTIONS:	

SITE NAME:	URL:
USERNAME:	PASSWORD:
EMAIL ADDRESS:	
NOTES / SECURITY QUESTIONS:	

P	
SITE NAME:	**URL:**
USERNAME:	**PASSWORD:**
EMAIL ADDRESS:	
NOTES / SECURITY QUESTIONS:	
SITE NAME:	**URL:**
USERNAME:	**PASSWORD:**
EMAIL ADDRESS:	
NOTES / SECURITY QUESTIONS:	
SITE NAME:	**URL:**
USERNAME:	**PASSWORD:**
EMAIL ADDRESS:	
NOTES / SECURITY QUESTIONS:	
SITE NAME:	**URL:**
USERNAME:	**PASSWORD:**
EMAIL ADDRESS:	
NOTES / SECURITY QUESTIONS:	

P

SITE NAME:	URL:
USERNAME:	PASSWORD:
EMAIL ADDRESS:	
NOTES / SECURITY QUESTIONS:	

SITE NAME:	URL:
USERNAME:	PASSWORD:
EMAIL ADDRESS:	
NOTES / SECURITY QUESTIONS:	

SITE NAME:	URL:
USERNAME:	PASSWORD:
EMAIL ADDRESS:	
NOTES / SECURITY QUESTIONS:	

SITE NAME:	URL:
USERNAME:	PASSWORD:
EMAIL ADDRESS:	
NOTES / SECURITY QUESTIONS:	

P

SITE NAME:	URL:
USERNAME:	PASSWORD:
EMAIL ADDRESS:	
NOTES / SECURITY QUESTIONS:	

SITE NAME:	URL:
USERNAME:	PASSWORD:
EMAIL ADDRESS:	
NOTES / SECURITY QUESTIONS:	

SITE NAME:	URL:
USERNAME:	PASSWORD:
EMAIL ADDRESS:	
NOTES / SECURITY QUESTIONS:	

SITE NAME:	URL:
USERNAME:	PASSWORD:
EMAIL ADDRESS:	
NOTES / SECURITY QUESTIONS:	

Q

SITE NAME:	URL:
USERNAME:	PASSWORD:
EMAIL ADDRESS:	
NOTES / SECURITY QUESTIONS:	

SITE NAME:	URL:
USERNAME:	PASSWORD:
EMAIL ADDRESS:	
NOTES / SECURITY QUESTIONS:	

SITE NAME:	URL:
USERNAME:	PASSWORD:
EMAIL ADDRESS:	
NOTES / SECURITY QUESTIONS:	

SITE NAME:	URL:
USERNAME:	PASSWORD:
EMAIL ADDRESS:	
NOTES / SECURITY QUESTIONS:	

Q

SITE NAME:	URL:
USERNAME:	PASSWORD:
EMAIL ADDRESS:	
NOTES / SECURITY QUESTIONS:	

SITE NAME:	URL:
USERNAME:	PASSWORD:
EMAIL ADDRESS:	
NOTES / SECURITY QUESTIONS:	

SITE NAME:	URL:
USERNAME:	PASSWORD:
EMAIL ADDRESS:	
NOTES / SECURITY QUESTIONS:	

SITE NAME:	URL:
USERNAME:	PASSWORD:
EMAIL ADDRESS:	
NOTES / SECURITY QUESTIONS:	

Q

SITE NAME:	URL:
USERNAME:	PASSWORD:
EMAIL ADDRESS:	
NOTES / SECURITY QUESTIONS:	

SITE NAME:	URL:
USERNAME:	PASSWORD:
EMAIL ADDRESS:	
NOTES / SECURITY QUESTIONS:	

SITE NAME:	URL:
USERNAME:	PASSWORD:
EMAIL ADDRESS:	
NOTES / SECURITY QUESTIONS:	

SITE NAME:	URL:
USERNAME:	PASSWORD:
EMAIL ADDRESS:	
NOTES / SECURITY QUESTIONS:	

Q

SITE NAME:	URL:
USERNAME:	PASSWORD:
EMAIL ADDRESS:	
NOTES / SECURITY QUESTIONS:	

SITE NAME:	URL:
USERNAME:	PASSWORD:
EMAIL ADDRESS:	
NOTES / SECURITY QUESTIONS:	

SITE NAME:	URL:
USERNAME:	PASSWORD:
EMAIL ADDRESS:	
NOTES / SECURITY QUESTIONS:	

SITE NAME:	URL:
USERNAME:	PASSWORD:
EMAIL ADDRESS:	
NOTES / SECURITY QUESTIONS:	

R

SITE NAME:	URL:
USERNAME:	PASSWORD:
EMAIL ADDRESS:	
NOTES / SECURITY QUESTIONS:	

SITE NAME:	URL:
USERNAME:	PASSWORD:
EMAIL ADDRESS:	
NOTES / SECURITY QUESTIONS:	

SITE NAME:	URL:
USERNAME:	PASSWORD:
EMAIL ADDRESS:	
NOTES / SECURITY QUESTIONS:	

SITE NAME:	URL:
USERNAME:	PASSWORD:
EMAIL ADDRESS:	
NOTES / SECURITY QUESTIONS:	

R

SITE NAME:	URL:
USERNAME:	PASSWORD:
EMAIL ADDRESS:	
NOTES / SECURITY QUESTIONS:	

SITE NAME:	URL:
USERNAME:	PASSWORD:
EMAIL ADDRESS:	
NOTES / SECURITY QUESTIONS:	

SITE NAME:	URL:
USERNAME:	PASSWORD:
EMAIL ADDRESS:	
NOTES / SECURITY QUESTIONS:	

SITE NAME:	URL:
USERNAME:	PASSWORD:
EMAIL ADDRESS:	
NOTES / SECURITY QUESTIONS:	

R

SITE NAME:	URL:
USERNAME:	PASSWORD:
EMAIL ADDRESS:	
NOTES / SECURITY QUESTIONS:	

SITE NAME:	URL:
USERNAME:	PASSWORD:
EMAIL ADDRESS:	
NOTES / SECURITY QUESTIONS:	

SITE NAME:	URL:
USERNAME:	PASSWORD:
EMAIL ADDRESS:	
NOTES / SECURITY QUESTIONS:	

SITE NAME:	URL:
USERNAME:	PASSWORD:
EMAIL ADDRESS:	
NOTES / SECURITY QUESTIONS:	

R

SITE NAME:	URL:
USERNAME:	PASSWORD:
EMAIL ADDRESS:	
NOTES / SECURITY QUESTIONS:	

SITE NAME:	URL:
USERNAME:	PASSWORD:
EMAIL ADDRESS:	
NOTES / SECURITY QUESTIONS:	

SITE NAME:	URL:
USERNAME:	PASSWORD:
EMAIL ADDRESS:	
NOTES / SECURITY QUESTIONS:	

SITE NAME:	URL:
USERNAME:	PASSWORD:
EMAIL ADDRESS:	
NOTES / SECURITY QUESTIONS:	

S

SITE NAME: | **URL:**
USERNAME: | **PASSWORD:**
EMAIL ADDRESS:
NOTES / SECURITY QUESTIONS:

SITE NAME: | **URL:**
USERNAME: | **PASSWORD:**
EMAIL ADDRESS:
NOTES / SECURITY QUESTIONS:

SITE NAME: | **URL:**
USERNAME: | **PASSWORD:**
EMAIL ADDRESS:
NOTES / SECURITY QUESTIONS:

SITE NAME: | **URL:**
USERNAME: | **PASSWORD:**
EMAIL ADDRESS:
NOTES / SECURITY QUESTIONS:

S

SITE NAME:	URL:
USERNAME:	PASSWORD:
EMAIL ADDRESS:	
NOTES / SECURITY QUESTIONS:	

SITE NAME:	URL:
USERNAME:	PASSWORD:
EMAIL ADDRESS:	
NOTES / SECURITY QUESTIONS:	

SITE NAME:	URL:
USERNAME:	PASSWORD:
EMAIL ADDRESS:	
NOTES / SECURITY QUESTIONS:	

SITE NAME:	URL:
USERNAME:	PASSWORD:
EMAIL ADDRESS:	
NOTES / SECURITY QUESTIONS:	

S

SITE NAME:	URL:
USERNAME:	PASSWORD:
EMAIL ADDRESS:	
NOTES / SECURITY QUESTIONS:	

SITE NAME:	URL:
USERNAME:	PASSWORD:
EMAIL ADDRESS:	
NOTES / SECURITY QUESTIONS:	

SITE NAME:	URL:
USERNAME:	PASSWORD:
EMAIL ADDRESS:	
NOTES / SECURITY QUESTIONS:	

SITE NAME:	URL:
USERNAME:	PASSWORD:
EMAIL ADDRESS:	
NOTES / SECURITY QUESTIONS:	

S

SITE NAME:	URL:
USERNAME:	PASSWORD:
EMAIL ADDRESS:	
NOTES / SECURITY QUESTIONS:	

SITE NAME:	URL:
USERNAME:	PASSWORD:
EMAIL ADDRESS:	
NOTES / SECURITY QUESTIONS:	

SITE NAME:	URL:
USERNAME:	PASSWORD:
EMAIL ADDRESS:	
NOTES / SECURITY QUESTIONS:	

SITE NAME:	URL:
USERNAME:	PASSWORD:
EMAIL ADDRESS:	
NOTES / SECURITY QUESTIONS:	

T

SITE NAME:	URL:
USERNAME:	PASSWORD:
EMAIL ADDRESS:	
NOTES / SECURITY QUESTIONS:	

SITE NAME:	URL:
USERNAME:	PASSWORD:
EMAIL ADDRESS:	
NOTES / SECURITY QUESTIONS:	

SITE NAME:	URL:
USERNAME:	PASSWORD:
EMAIL ADDRESS:	
NOTES / SECURITY QUESTIONS:	

SITE NAME:	URL:
USERNAME:	PASSWORD:
EMAIL ADDRESS:	
NOTES / SECURITY QUESTIONS:	

T	

SITE NAME:	URL:
USERNAME:	PASSWORD:
EMAIL ADDRESS:	
NOTES / SECURITY QUESTIONS:	

SITE NAME:	URL:
USERNAME:	PASSWORD:
EMAIL ADDRESS:	
NOTES / SECURITY QUESTIONS:	

SITE NAME:	URL:
USERNAME:	PASSWORD:
EMAIL ADDRESS:	
NOTES / SECURITY QUESTIONS:	

SITE NAME:	URL:
USERNAME:	PASSWORD:
EMAIL ADDRESS:	
NOTES / SECURITY QUESTIONS:	

T

SITE NAME:	URL:
USERNAME:	PASSWORD:
EMAIL ADDRESS:	
NOTES / SECURITY QUESTIONS:	

SITE NAME:	URL:
USERNAME:	PASSWORD:
EMAIL ADDRESS:	
NOTES / SECURITY QUESTIONS:	

SITE NAME:	URL:
USERNAME:	PASSWORD:
EMAIL ADDRESS:	
NOTES / SECURITY QUESTIONS:	

SITE NAME:	URL:
USERNAME:	PASSWORD:
EMAIL ADDRESS:	
NOTES / SECURITY QUESTIONS:	

T

SITE NAME:	URL:
USERNAME:	PASSWORD:
EMAIL ADDRESS:	
NOTES / SECURITY QUESTIONS:	

SITE NAME:	URL:
USERNAME:	PASSWORD:
EMAIL ADDRESS:	
NOTES / SECURITY QUESTIONS:	

SITE NAME:	URL:
USERNAME:	PASSWORD:
EMAIL ADDRESS:	
NOTES / SECURITY QUESTIONS:	

SITE NAME:	URL:
USERNAME:	PASSWORD:
EMAIL ADDRESS:	
NOTES / SECURITY QUESTIONS:	

U

SITE NAME:	URL:
USERNAME:	PASSWORD:
EMAIL ADDRESS:	
NOTES / SECURITY QUESTIONS:	

SITE NAME:	URL:
USERNAME:	PASSWORD:
EMAIL ADDRESS:	
NOTES / SECURITY QUESTIONS:	

SITE NAME:	URL:
USERNAME:	PASSWORD:
EMAIL ADDRESS:	
NOTES / SECURITY QUESTIONS:	

SITE NAME:	URL:
USERNAME:	PASSWORD:
EMAIL ADDRESS:	
NOTES / SECURITY QUESTIONS:	

U

SITE NAME:	URL:
USERNAME:	PASSWORD:
EMAIL ADDRESS:	
NOTES / SECURITY QUESTIONS:	

SITE NAME:	URL:
USERNAME:	PASSWORD:
EMAIL ADDRESS:	
NOTES / SECURITY QUESTIONS:	

SITE NAME:	URL:
USERNAME:	PASSWORD:
EMAIL ADDRESS:	
NOTES / SECURITY QUESTIONS:	

SITE NAME:	URL:
USERNAME:	PASSWORD:
EMAIL ADDRESS:	
NOTES / SECURITY QUESTIONS:	

U

SITE NAME:	URL:
USERNAME:	PASSWORD:
EMAIL ADDRESS:	
NOTES / SECURITY QUESTIONS:	

SITE NAME:	URL:
USERNAME:	PASSWORD:
EMAIL ADDRESS:	
NOTES / SECURITY QUESTIONS:	

SITE NAME:	URL:
USERNAME:	PASSWORD:
EMAIL ADDRESS:	
NOTES / SECURITY QUESTIONS:	

SITE NAME:	URL:
USERNAME:	PASSWORD:
EMAIL ADDRESS:	
NOTES / SECURITY QUESTIONS:	

U

SITE NAME:	URL:
USERNAME:	PASSWORD:
EMAIL ADDRESS:	
NOTES / SECURITY QUESTIONS:	

SITE NAME:	URL:
USERNAME:	PASSWORD:
EMAIL ADDRESS:	
NOTES / SECURITY QUESTIONS:	

SITE NAME:	URL:
USERNAME:	PASSWORD:
EMAIL ADDRESS:	
NOTES / SECURITY QUESTIONS:	

SITE NAME:	URL:
USERNAME:	PASSWORD:
EMAIL ADDRESS:	
NOTES / SECURITY QUESTIONS:	

V

SITE NAME:	URL:
USERNAME:	PASSWORD:
EMAIL ADDRESS:	
NOTES / SECURITY QUESTIONS:	

SITE NAME:	URL:
USERNAME:	PASSWORD:
EMAIL ADDRESS:	
NOTES / SECURITY QUESTIONS:	

SITE NAME:	URL:
USERNAME:	PASSWORD:
EMAIL ADDRESS:	
NOTES / SECURITY QUESTIONS:	

SITE NAME:	URL:
USERNAME:	PASSWORD:
EMAIL ADDRESS:	
NOTES / SECURITY QUESTIONS:	

V

SITE NAME:	URL:
USERNAME:	PASSWORD:
EMAIL ADDRESS:	
NOTES / SECURITY QUESTIONS:	

SITE NAME:	URL:
USERNAME:	PASSWORD:
EMAIL ADDRESS:	
NOTES / SECURITY QUESTIONS:	

SITE NAME:	URL:
USERNAME:	PASSWORD:
EMAIL ADDRESS:	
NOTES / SECURITY QUESTIONS:	

SITE NAME:	URL:
USERNAME:	PASSWORD:
EMAIL ADDRESS:	
NOTES / SECURITY QUESTIONS:	

V

SITE NAME:	URL:
USERNAME:	PASSWORD:
EMAIL ADDRESS:	
NOTES / SECURITY QUESTIONS:	

SITE NAME:	URL:
USERNAME:	PASSWORD:
EMAIL ADDRESS:	
NOTES / SECURITY QUESTIONS:	

SITE NAME:	URL:
USERNAME:	PASSWORD:
EMAIL ADDRESS:	
NOTES / SECURITY QUESTIONS:	

SITE NAME:	URL:
USERNAME:	PASSWORD:
EMAIL ADDRESS:	
NOTES / SECURITY QUESTIONS:	

V

SITE NAME:	URL:
USERNAME:	PASSWORD:
EMAIL ADDRESS:	
NOTES / SECURITY QUESTIONS:	

SITE NAME:	URL:
USERNAME:	PASSWORD:
EMAIL ADDRESS:	
NOTES / SECURITY QUESTIONS:	

SITE NAME:	URL:
USERNAME:	PASSWORD:
EMAIL ADDRESS:	
NOTES / SECURITY QUESTIONS:	

SITE NAME:	URL:
USERNAME:	PASSWORD:
EMAIL ADDRESS:	
NOTES / SECURITY QUESTIONS:	

W

SITE NAME:	URL:
USERNAME:	PASSWORD:
EMAIL ADDRESS:	
NOTES / SECURITY QUESTIONS:	

SITE NAME:	URL:
USERNAME:	PASSWORD:
EMAIL ADDRESS:	
NOTES / SECURITY QUESTIONS:	

SITE NAME:	URL:
USERNAME:	PASSWORD:
EMAIL ADDRESS:	
NOTES / SECURITY QUESTIONS:	

SITE NAME:	URL:
USERNAME:	PASSWORD:
EMAIL ADDRESS:	
NOTES / SECURITY QUESTIONS:	

W

SITE NAME:	URL:
USERNAME:	PASSWORD:
EMAIL ADDRESS:	
NOTES / SECURITY QUESTIONS:	

SITE NAME:	URL:
USERNAME:	PASSWORD:
EMAIL ADDRESS:	
NOTES / SECURITY QUESTIONS:	

SITE NAME:	URL:
USERNAME:	PASSWORD:
EMAIL ADDRESS:	
NOTES / SECURITY QUESTIONS:	

SITE NAME:	URL:
USERNAME:	PASSWORD:
EMAIL ADDRESS:	
NOTES / SECURITY QUESTIONS:	

X

SITE NAME:	URL:
USERNAME:	PASSWORD:
EMAIL ADDRESS:	
NOTES / SECURITY QUESTIONS:	

SITE NAME:	URL:
USERNAME:	PASSWORD:
EMAIL ADDRESS:	
NOTES / SECURITY QUESTIONS:	

SITE NAME:	URL:
USERNAME:	PASSWORD:
EMAIL ADDRESS:	
NOTES / SECURITY QUESTIONS:	

SITE NAME:	URL:
USERNAME:	PASSWORD:
EMAIL ADDRESS:	
NOTES / SECURITY QUESTIONS:	

X

SITE NAME:	URL:
USERNAME:	PASSWORD:
EMAIL ADDRESS:	
NOTES / SECURITY QUESTIONS:	

SITE NAME:	URL:
USERNAME:	PASSWORD:
EMAIL ADDRESS:	
NOTES / SECURITY QUESTIONS:	

SITE NAME:	URL:
USERNAME:	PASSWORD:
EMAIL ADDRESS:	
NOTES / SECURITY QUESTIONS:	

SITE NAME:	URL:
USERNAME:	PASSWORD:
EMAIL ADDRESS:	
NOTES / SECURITY QUESTIONS:	

Y

SITE NAME:	URL:
USERNAME:	PASSWORD:
EMAIL ADDRESS:	
NOTES / SECURITY QUESTIONS:	

SITE NAME:	URL:
USERNAME:	PASSWORD:
EMAIL ADDRESS:	
NOTES / SECURITY QUESTIONS:	

SITE NAME:	URL:
USERNAME:	PASSWORD:
EMAIL ADDRESS:	
NOTES / SECURITY QUESTIONS:	

SITE NAME:	URL:
USERNAME:	PASSWORD:
EMAIL ADDRESS:	
NOTES / SECURITY QUESTIONS:	

Y

SITE NAME:	URL:
USERNAME:	PASSWORD:
EMAIL ADDRESS:	
NOTES / SECURITY QUESTIONS:	

SITE NAME:	URL:
USERNAME:	PASSWORD:
EMAIL ADDRESS:	
NOTES / SECURITY QUESTIONS:	

SITE NAME:	URL:
USERNAME:	PASSWORD:
EMAIL ADDRESS:	
NOTES / SECURITY QUESTIONS:	

SITE NAME:	URL:
USERNAME:	PASSWORD:
EMAIL ADDRESS:	
NOTES / SECURITY QUESTIONS:	

Z

SITE NAME: | **URL:**

USERNAME: | **PASSWORD:**

EMAIL ADDRESS:

NOTES / SECURITY QUESTIONS:

SITE NAME: | **URL:**

USERNAME: | **PASSWORD:**

EMAIL ADDRESS:

NOTES / SECURITY QUESTIONS:

SITE NAME: | **URL:**

USERNAME: | **PASSWORD:**

EMAIL ADDRESS:

NOTES / SECURITY QUESTIONS:

SITE NAME: | **URL:**

USERNAME: | **PASSWORD:**

EMAIL ADDRESS:

NOTES / SECURITY QUESTIONS:

Z

SITE NAME:	URL:
USERNAME:	PASSWORD:
EMAIL ADDRESS:	
NOTES / SECURITY QUESTIONS:	

SITE NAME:	URL:
USERNAME:	PASSWORD:
EMAIL ADDRESS:	
NOTES / SECURITY QUESTIONS:	

SITE NAME:	URL:
USERNAME:	PASSWORD:
EMAIL ADDRESS:	
NOTES / SECURITY QUESTIONS:	

SITE NAME:	URL:
USERNAME:	PASSWORD:
EMAIL ADDRESS:	
NOTES / SECURITY QUESTIONS:	

0-9

SITE NAME: | **URL:**

USERNAME: | **PASSWORD:**

EMAIL ADDRESS:

NOTES / SECURITY QUESTIONS:

SITE NAME: | **URL:**

USERNAME: | **PASSWORD:**

EMAIL ADDRESS:

NOTES / SECURITY QUESTIONS:

SITE NAME: | **URL:**

USERNAME: | **PASSWORD:**

EMAIL ADDRESS:

NOTES / SECURITY QUESTIONS:

SITE NAME: | **URL:**

USERNAME: | **PASSWORD:**

EMAIL ADDRESS:

NOTES / SECURITY QUESTIONS:

0-9

SITE NAME:	URL:
USERNAME:	PASSWORD:
EMAIL ADDRESS:	
NOTES / SECURITY QUESTIONS:	

SITE NAME:	URL:
USERNAME:	PASSWORD:
EMAIL ADDRESS:	
NOTES / SECURITY QUESTIONS:	

SITE NAME:	URL:
USERNAME:	PASSWORD:
EMAIL ADDRESS:	
NOTES / SECURITY QUESTIONS:	

SITE NAME:	URL:
USERNAME:	PASSWORD:
EMAIL ADDRESS:	
NOTES / SECURITY QUESTIONS:	

INTERNET RECORDS

EMAIL ADDRESS:				
USERNAME:				
PASSWORD:				
MAIL SERVER:	POP ☐		IMAP ☐	
INCOMING MAIL:			PORT:	
USERNAME:				
PASSWORD:				
OUTGOING MAIL:			PORT:	
USERNAME:				
PASSWORD:				
NOTES:				

EMAIL ADDRESS:				
USERNAME:				
PASSWORD:				
MAIL SERVER:	POP ☐		IMAP ☐	
INCOMING MAIL:			PORT:	
USERNAME:				
PASSWORD:				
OUTGOING MAIL:			PORT:	
USERNAME:				
PASSWORD:				
NOTES:				

INTERNET RECORDS

EMAIL ADDRESS:				
USERNAME:				
PASSWORD:				
MAIL SERVER:	POP ☐		IMAP ☐	
INCOMING MAIL:			PORT:	
USERNAME:				
PASSWORD:				
OUTGOING MAIL:			PORT:	
USERNAME:				
PASSWORD:				
NOTES:				

EMAIL ADDRESS:				
USERNAME:				
PASSWORD:				
MAIL SERVER:	POP ☐		IMAP ☐	
INCOMING MAIL:			PORT:	
USERNAME:				
PASSWORD:				
OUTGOING MAIL:			PORT:	
USERNAME:				
PASSWORD:				
NOTES:				

INTERNET RECORDS

WIFI NETWORK:	
PASSWORD:	
NOTES:	
WIFI NETWORK:	
PASSWORD:	
NOTES:	
WIFI NETWORK:	
PASSWORD:	
NOTES:	
WIFI NETWORK:	
PASSWORD:	
NOTES:	
WIFI NETWORK:	
PASSWORD:	
NOTES:	
WIFI NETWORK:	
PASSWORD:	
NOTES:	
WIFI NETWORK:	
PASSWORD:	
NOTES:	

INTERNET RECORDS

WIFI NETWORK:	
PASSWORD:	
NOTES:	
WIFI NETWORK:	
PASSWORD:	
NOTES:	
WIFI NETWORK:	
PASSWORD:	
NOTES:	
WIFI NETWORK:	
PASSWORD:	
NOTES:	
WIFI NETWORK:	
PASSWORD:	
NOTES:	
WIFI NETWORK:	
PASSWORD:	
NOTES:	
WIFI NETWORK:	
PASSWORD:	
NOTES:	

INTERNET RECORDS

WIFI NETWORK:
PASSWORD:
NOTES:
WIFI NETWORK:
PASSWORD:
NOTES:
WIFI NETWORK:
PASSWORD:
NOTES:
WIFI NETWORK:
PASSWORD:
NOTES:
WIFI NETWORK:
PASSWORD:
NOTES:
WIFI NETWORK:
PASSWORD:
NOTES:
WIFI NETWORK:
PASSWORD:
NOTES:

INTERNET RECORDS

WIFI NETWORK:
PASSWORD:
NOTES:
WIFI NETWORK:
PASSWORD:
NOTES:
WIFI NETWORK:
PASSWORD:
NOTES:
WIFI NETWORK:
PASSWORD:
NOTES:
WIFI NETWORK:
PASSWORD:
NOTES:
WIFI NETWORK:
PASSWORD:
NOTES:
WIFI NETWORK:
PASSWORD:
NOTES:

DATA RECORDS

PROTECTED FILE NAME:
PASSWORD / KEY:
PROTECTED FILE NAME:
PASSWORD / KEY:
PROTECTED FILE NAME:
PASSWORD / KEY:
PROTECTED FILE NAME:
PASSWORD / KEY:
PROTECTED FILE NAME:
PASSWORD / KEY:
PROTECTED FILE NAME:
PASSWORD / KEY:
PROTECTED FILE NAME:
PASSWORD / KEY:
PROTECTED FILE NAME:
PASSWORD / KEY:
PROTECTED FILE NAME:
PASSWORD / KEY:
PROTECTED FILE NAME:
PASSWORD / KEY:
PROTECTED FILE NAME:
PASSWORD KEY:

DATA RECORDS

PROTECTED FILE NAME:
PASSWORD / KEY:
PROTECTED FILE NAME:
PASSWORD / KEY:
PROTECTED FILE NAME:
PASSWORD / KEY:
PROTECTED FILE NAME:
PASSWORD / KEY:
PROTECTED FILE NAME:
PASSWORD / KEY:
PROTECTED FILE NAME:
PASSWORD / KEY:
PROTECTED FILE NAME:
PASSWORD / KEY:
PROTECTED FILE NAME:
PASSWORD / KEY:
PROTECTED FILE NAME:
PASSWORD / KEY:
PROTECTED FILE NAME:
PASSWORD / KEY:
PROTECTED FILE NAME:
PASSWORD KEY:

COMPUTER RECORDS

HOME ROUTER

WIRELESS NETWORK NAME (SSID):

WIRELESS PASSWORD:

ROUTER LOGIN URL:

LOGIN USERNAME:

LOGIN PASSWORD:

SERIAL #:

WORK ROUTER

WIRELESS NETWORK NAME (SSID):

WIRELESS PASSWORD:

ROUTER LOGIN URL:

LOGIN USERNAME:

LOGIN PASSWORD:

SERIAL #:

OTHER ROUTER

WIRELESS NETWORK NAME (SSID):

WIRELESS PASSWORD:

ROUTER LOGIN URL:

LOGIN USERNAME:

LOGIN PASSWORD:

SERIAL #:

COMPUTER RECORDS

HOME COMPUTER

BRAND / MODEL:

SERIAL #:

NOTEBOOK COMPUTER

BRAND / MODEL:

SERIAL #:

TABLET

BRAND / MODEL:

SERIAL #:

MOBILE

BRAND / MODEL:

SERIAL #:

OTHER DEVICE

BRAND / MODEL:

SERIAL #:

OTHER DEVICE

BRAND / MODEL:

SERIAL #:

COMPUTER RECORDS

OPERATING SYSTEM:

LICENSE KEY / CODE:

OPERATING SYSTEM:

LICENSE KEY / CODE:

APP NAME:

LICENSE KEY / CODE:

APP NAME:

LICENSE KEY / CODE:

APP NAME:

LICENSE KEY / CODE:

APP NAME:

LICENSE KEY / CODE:

APP NAME:

LICENSE KEY / CODE:

APP NAME:

LICENSE KEY / CODE:

APP NAME:

LICENSE KEY / CODE:

APP NAME:

LICENSE KEY / CODE:

COMPUTER RECORDS

APP NAME:

LICENSE KEY / CODE:

APP NAME:

LICENSE KEY / CODE:

APP NAME:

LICENSE KEY / CODE:

APP NAME:

LICENSE KEY / CODE:

APP NAME:

LICENSE KEY / CODE:

APP NAME:

LICENSE KEY / CODE:

APP NAME:

LICENSE KEY / CODE:

APP NAME:

LICENSE KEY / CODE:

APP NAME:

LICENSE KEY / CODE:

APP NAME:

LICENSE KEY / CODE:

APP NAME:

LICENSE KEY / CODE:

www.ingramcontent.com/pod-product-compliance
Lightning Source LLC
Chambersburg PA
CBHW071005050326
40689CB00014B/3499